ACX-1344

cap

D0793327

4/05CAP

THE *Pennsylvania* COLONY

Our Thirteen Colonies

SPIRIT
of America®

THE *Pennsylvania* COLONY

By Jean Kinney Williams

*Content Adviser: Eric Gilg, Department of History, University of
Massachusetts, Amherst, Massachusetts*

The
**Child's
World**®

The Child's World®
Chanhassen, Minnesota

6

THE *Pennsylvania* COLONY

Published in the United States of America by The Child's World®
PO Box 326 • Chanhassen, MN 55317-0326 • 800-599-READ • www.childsworld.com

Acknowledgments
The Child's World®: Mary Berendes, Publishing Director

Editorial Directions, Inc.: E. Russell Primm, Editorial Director; Melissa McDaniel, Line Editor; Elizabeth K. Martin, Assistant Editor; Olivia Nellums, Editorial Assistant; Susan Hindman, Copy Editor; Joanne Mattern, Proofreader; Kevin Cunningham, Peter Garnham, Ruthanne Swiatkowski, Fact Checkers; Tim Griffin/IndexServ, Indexer; Cian Loughlin O'Day, Photo Researcher; Linda S. Koutris, Photo Selector

Photo
Cover: North Wind Picture Archives; Bettmann/Corbis: 16, 20, 22, 27, 34; Bridgeman Art Library/Pennsylvania Academy of Fine Arts: 28; Corbis: 6 (David Muench), 8 (Nathan Benn), 21, 35 (Patrick Ward); Getty Images/Hulton Archive: 9, 10, 11, 12, 13, 14, 15, 18, 23, 24, 26; Getty Images/Time Life Pictures: 17; North Wind Picture Archives: 32; Stock Montage: 25, 29, 30, 33.

Registration
The Child's World®, Spirit of America®, and their associated logos are the sole property and registered trademarks of The Child's World®.

Library of Congress Cataloging-in-Publication Data
Williams, Jean Kinney.
  The Pennsylvania Colony / by Jean Kinney Williams.
    p. cm. — (Our colonies)
"Spirit of America."
Summary: Relates the history of the Colony of Pennsylvania from its founding by William Penn in 1681 to statehood in 1787. Includes bibliographical references (p.) and index.
  ISBN 1-56766-684-1 (alk. paper)
  1. Pennsylvania—History—Colonial period, ca. 1600–1775—Juvenile literature. 2. Pennsylvania—History—1775–1865—Juvenile literature. [1. Pennsylvania—History—Colonial period, ca. 1600–1775. 2. Pennsylvania—History—1775–1865.] I. Title. II. Series.
  F152.W57 2003
  973.8'02—dc21   2003003774

12   24   29

Contents

Chapter ONE

The Original People

Native Americans lived along the Delaware River and Delaware Bay long before Europeans arrived in the area.

WHEN THE FIRST EUROPEANS ARRIVED IN WHAT is now Pennsylvania, many people were already living there. The people who lived along Delaware Bay and the Delaware River called themselves the Lenni-Lenape, meaning "the original people."

Many Native American groups lived in what would become Pennsylvania. The Nanticoke and the Shawnee lived in eastern Pennsylvania. The Erie and the Monongahela lived in what is now western Pennsylvania. The Susquehanna, who lived in central Pennsylvania, were an Iroquois people. Several other Iroquois

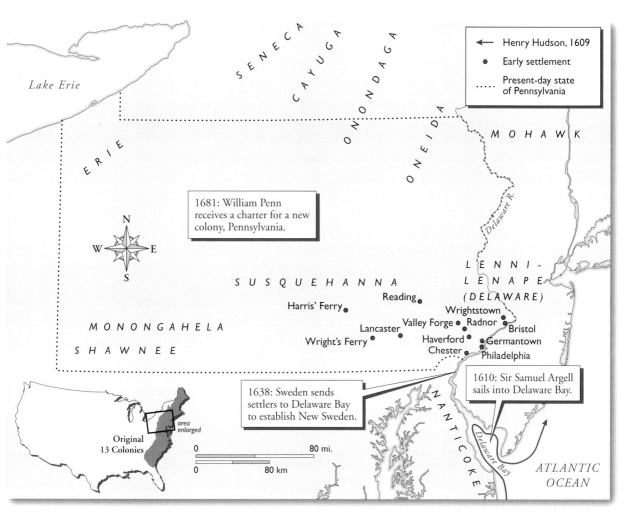

Pennsylvania Colony at the time of the first European settlement

groups from New York, Canada, and Pennsylvania banded together in what was called the Five Nations. Later, the Tuscarora from North Carolina also joined the group to make it the Six Nations. The aggressive Iroquois conquered many of the Northeast's Native Americans. They ruled the fur trade with Europeans by working with each other and fighting other native groups and white settlers.

7

The Lenni-Lenape and Iroquois lived in longhouses, like this traditional Iroquois longhouse.

The Lenni-Lenape managed to stay independent from most of these wars. They were generally friendly toward the early white settlers. They lived by farming, growing crops such as corn, beans, and squash. The Lenni-Lenape had a strong community life. Family groups lived together in a **longhouse,** which was between 30 and 100 feet (9 and 31 meters) long. Families were organized along the mother's line. For example, one longhouse might house a woman, her husband, their children, her daughters' families (if the daughters were married), and her parents. Lenni-Lenape villages operated independently. Each had its own leader who

8

made decisions based on input from all the village members.

The Iroquois also farmed and lived in longhouses. But unlike the Lenni-Lenape, they spent much of their time preparing for war. Iroquois women farmed and handled the duties of everyday life. Iroquois villages were in close contact with each other. Many of the paths the Iroquois used to travel between villages became important roads in Pennsylvania.

The Iroquois fought with the Susquehanna and pushed them out of southeastern Pennsylvania. But the Susquehanna suffered much more from their contact with Europeans. The first European explorers and settlers had brought diseases such as smallpox and measles to America. The Native Americans had never before been exposed to these diseases, so their bodies could not fight them. In 1658,

The Iroquois farmed but also spent much time preparing for war. An Iroquois warrior is pictured above.

9

Their first contacts with Europeans exposed Native Americans to many diseases, such as smallpox.

smallpox swept through the Susquehanna, killing almost all of them. By 1675, the few Susquehanna still alive had gone to live with other native groups. Across North America, millions of Native Americans were killed by disease in the years after Europeans first arrived.

THE LENNI-LENAPE WERE A RELIGIOUS PEOPLE, AS WERE ALL NATIVE AMERICANS. They believed in a creator, the Great Spirit, who would judge them when they died. They also believed in less-powerful gods who ruled over the Earth, such as the Thunderers, who came in storm clouds to bring rain for the crops. They believed that all things on Earth had souls: animals, water, trees, and even rocks.

Like people of many faiths, the Lenni-Lenape taught the "Golden Rule," to treat others as you want to be treated. Many Lenni-Lenape accepted Christianity. But they still had trouble with Europeans because, as one said, many "did not act according to the good words which they told us." In other words, the white settlers didn't always practice what they preached.

Chapter TWO

The Beginning of Pennsylvania

Samuel Argell sailed into and named Delaware Bay in 1610. The surrounding area attracted many settlers in the years that followed.

I N 1610, E NGLISHMAN S AMUEL A RGELL SAILED into Delaware Bay looking for food for the starving people of Jamestown, Virginia. He named the bay after Virginia's governor, Lord De La Warre. Delaware became the name of the bay and the river flowing into it. Within a few years, Dutch traders were living in the region.

Around 1638, a band of Swedish settlers created Pennsylvania's first permanent white settlement. They bought land from the Lenni-Lenape and built a fort. Their governor lived in a two-story log home near present-day Philadelphia.

But the Dutch still were interested in Delaware Bay. In 1655, 600 Dutch soldiers arrived there. The Swedes were greatly outnumbered. They gave up control of the area, though most of the Swedish settlers continued to live there. The Dutch did little in the area, however, and by 1664 the English were in charge. It was Englishman William Penn who turned the Delaware River region into a bustling colony.

Back in England, a new religious group called the Quakers was always in trouble with the government. William Penn was a Quaker leader. His father was a wealthy and important navy officer who knew King Charles II. In 1681, Charles gave Penn a **charter** for a new colony in America, which would be called Pennsylvania. William Penn had wanted to name it Sylvania, which means "forest." King Charles added Penn to the name in honor of William Penn's father. Now Quakers had a place to go to practice their religion in peace.

Quakers were humble people who

Interesting Fact

▶ In 1682, Penn's first charter for Pennsylvania, said that all children in the colony should know how to read and write by age 12.

A group of Quakers, also known as the Religious Society of Friends, holds a meeting. William Penn was a Quaker leader.

13

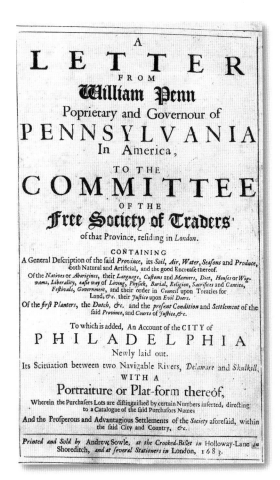

A LETTER FROM William Penn Poprietary and Governour of PENNSYLVANIA In America, TO THE COMMITTEE OF THE Free Society of Traders of that Province, residing in London.

CONTAINING

A General Description of the said Province, its Soil, Air, Water, Seasons and Produce, both Natural and Artificial, and the good Encrease thereof.

Of the Natives or Aborigines, their Language, Customs and Manners, Diet, Houses or Wigwams, Liberality, easie way of Living, Physick, Burial, Religion, Sacrifices and Cantico, Festivals, Government, and their order in Council upon Treaties for Land, &c. their Justice upon Evil Doers.

Of the first Planters, the Dutch, &c. and the present Condition and Settlement of the said Province, and Courts of Justice, &c.

To which is added, An Account of the CITY of PHILADELPHIA Newly laid out.

Its Scituation between two Navigable Rivers, Delaware and Skulkill,

WITH A

Portraiture or Plat-form thereof,

Wherein the Purchasers Lots are distinguished by certain Numbers inserted, directing to a Catalogue of the said Purchasors Names

And the Prosperous and Advantagious Settlements of the Society aforesaid, within the said City and Country, &c.

Printed and Sold by Andrew Sowle, at the Crooked-Billet in Holloway-Lane in Shoreditch, and at several Stationers in London, 1683.

William Penn distributed pamphlets to encourage people to settle in Pennsylvania.

didn't consider a king more important than a servant. They believed that everyone was equal in God's eyes. They valued honesty, hard work, and education. The Quakers took these qualities to Pennsylvania to try what Penn called his "holy experiment."

To lure settlers to Pennsylvania, Penn sent **pamphlets** around Europe advertising his new colony. "Let men be good, and the government cannot be bad," Penn wrote. There would be schools for all children in Penn's colony.

Penn's cousin William Markham was sent to Pennsylvania to meet with the Swedish and Dutch settlers there. Markham read them a letter in which Penn told them, "You shall be governed by laws of your own making." Penn insisted on respectful relations with the Native Americans, and he bought land from them. Penn's honesty was one reason the Lenni-Lenape and the new settlers had many years of peace.

IN WILLIAM PENN'S TIME, EUROPEAN KINGS CLAIMED THAT GOD GAVE THEM the right to rule. This meant that everyone had to obey them. The Quakers' belief in the equality of all people angered English leaders. Quakers also did not believe in war. This caused them trouble when the English army needed soldiers.

William Penn could have enjoyed great power or had a career in the military like his father. But he chose to be a Quaker and went to jail many times for it. He was still a Quaker when he became proprietor, or owner, of Pennsylvania. He owned more English land than anyone except the king.

The name of Pennsylvania's main city, Philadelphia, shows Penn's hope for humanity—in Greek it means "city of brotherly love."

Penn attracted thousands of settlers to Pennsylvania. He planned to support his family on the rent they owed him. But for 20 years, his property manager cheated him. At age 64, Penn spent months in prison in England because he could not pay his debts. He died 10 years later, having spent his fortune on the colony. Although Penn had no way of knowing it, many of his most basic beliefs would later be at the heart of a new nation.

Chapter THREE

The Growing Colony

As Pennsylvania's founder, Penn created a government for the new colony and designed the city of Philadelphia.

WILLIAM PENN CREATED A GOVERNMENT FOR Pennsylvania that included a governor, a council, and a general **assembly,** which was made up of representatives from around the colony. They all shared lawmaking responsibilities. By 1701, when Penn wrote the state's **constitution,** the assembly had taken over much of the lawmaking power. The

governor still had some power, and the council advised him.

The first wave of settlers to follow Penn were English Quakers. They settled in and around Philadelphia. For many years, they controlled the colony's government. By 1710, German-speaking people were fleeing to Pennsylvania from war-torn Europe. Many were skilled farmers. They turned Pennsylvania's fertile land into the "breadbasket" of the colonies. Pennsylvania farmers produced wheat, corn, and flax, which is used to make linen cloth.

Soon, Scotch-Irish people from northern Ireland were arriving in Pennsylvania. Much of the best farmland along the Delaware River was taken. So the fiercely independent Scotch-Irish headed west, settling on land that belonged to the Native Americans. They weren't interested in dealing peacefully with the native people.

In 1737, Penn's son Thomas made relations with the Native Americans even worse.

Thomas Penn cheated the Native Americans out of more land than the Lenni-Lenape intended to sell.

A view of Second Street in Philadelphia from the late 1700s

By then, he and his brothers were proprietors of Pennsylvania. Thomas wanted to buy more Lenni-Lenape land. He agreed to buy as much as a man could cover by walking for three days. This was called a walking purchase. But Penn hired runners and cheated the Lenni-Lenape out of much more land than they wanted to sell.

Pennsylvania was also home to many enslaved Africans. By 1730, 4,000 enslaved people had been brought to the colony. They usually worked alongside their owners at farming or in trades like sail-making or carpentry. At first many Quakers, including William Penn, owned slaves. But over time, the Quakers came to oppose slavery. In 1780, Pennsylvania became one of the first colonies to vote to gradually end slavery. By 1790, about 6,300 of Pennsylvania's 10,000 African-Americans were free.

All the while, Philadelphia was growing quickly. It was an orderly city, with a

18

neat pattern of wide, paved streets. People built brick and stone homes. The city had a good harbor, and its hardworking Quaker merchants and ship-builders became wealthy.

In May 1753, George Washington led an attack on French soldiers at this site, known as Jumonville Rocks, in Pennsylvania. Some historians consider this attack to be the beginning of the French and Indian War.

Even so, all of the homes in early Philadelphia were of similar sizes. The Quakers did not believe in showing off their wealth. Philadelphia benefited from Quaker beliefs. It had schools for African-American children and more decent prisons than other colonies. As Quaker influence faded in the 1700s, mansions and taverns became more common in the city.

By the mid-1700s, Philadelphia was the biggest city in the American colonies. Only Massachusetts had more people than Pennsylvania.

Meanwhile, Britain and France were competing for America's western lands. They fought over these lands in the French and Indian War, which began in 1754. The French encouraged the Lenni-Lenape to attack settlers in western Pennsylvania. Over the years,

Interesting Fact

▶ The mail service wasn't very reliable in the early 1700s. The **Continental Congress** put Benjamin Franklin, the postmaster of Philadelphia, in charge of all the mail in the colonies. Franklin greatly improved the mail system.

Chief Pontiac of the Ottawa led an attack against the white settlers who ignored treaties and settled on Native American lands.

Quakers in the assembly had refused to pay for military defense, leaving western Pennsylvania open to attack. But printer-turned-politician Benjamin Franklin helped resolve the issue, and the assembly approved money for the war. In 1763, Great Britain won the war, and with it all the land east of the Mississippi River.

Soon, another Native American war broke out in the west. In 1758, the British and the Native Americans had signed an agreement stating that all white settlers would stay east of the Susquehanna River. That agreement was often ignored. A small army led by Pontiac, an Ottawa leader, attacked some settlers. Pontiac wanted to push all white settlers back to the ocean. He didn't succeed, but many people, both whites and Native Americans, were killed during the war.

In 1763, the British government told settlers in Pennsylvania to follow the 1758 agreement by staying east of the Susquehanna. That way, the British army wouldn't have to build forts every time settlers moved farther west. That enraged the western settlers. They were very independent and didn't like getting orders from the government.

In 1765, another British action angered eastern Pennsylvanians. The French and Indian War had been very expensive. To raise money, the British **Parliament** passed the Stamp Act. This law said that anyone writing or printing a document had to buy a special stamp for the paper. Philadelphia's many lawyers, publishers, and businesspeople were furious. All across the colonies, people protested the Stamp Act by **boycotting** English goods shipped into the colonies. The boycott worked. Parliament ended the law less than a year later.

Then came the Townshend Acts. Britain charged colonists an extra tax on products like tea, paper, and glass that were shipped to the colonies. Again, the colonists began a boycott. Again, it worked. The taxes were lifted on everything except tea.

Colonists were getting fed up with English rules and taxes. They had no voice in Parliament. Some said it was time to go beyond boycotts—it was time for independence.

Interesting Fact

▸ The Sons of Liberty came together to make active protest against the Stamp Act. They burned the stamps, published newspaper articles against it, and threatened stamp agents. A tree in which they hung a doll resembling a stamp agent became known as the "Liberty Tree."

Published in October 1765, this paper is filled with cartoons and articles protesting the Stamp Act.

BENJAMIN FRANKLIN WAS ONE OF THE MOST REMARKABLE PEOPLE IN THE colonies. Born in Boston in 1706, he moved to Philadelphia as a teenager. He started his career as a printer, but became famous as a writer, scientist, community leader, and statesman. Every year for 26 years, he published *Poor Richard's Almanack,* one of the colonies' most popular books. In these books, a wise but poor farmer named Richard Saunders tells jokes and gives readers advice such as, "Early to bed, early to rise, makes a man healthy, wealthy, and wise."

Franklin was able to retire on the money he earned from these books. Then he turned his attention to science, politics, and city affairs. Franklin organized Philadelphia's first police force

Poor Richard, 1733.

AN
Almanack

For the Year of Chrift

1733,

Being the Firſt after LEAP YEAR:

And makes ſince the Creation	Years
By the Account of the Eastern *Greeks*	7241
By the Latin Church, when ☉ ent. ♈	6932
By the Computation of *W. W.*	5742
By the *Roman* Chronology	5682
By the *Jewish* Rabbies	5494

Wherein is contained

The Lunations, Eclipſes, Judgment of the Weather, Spring Tides, Planets Motions & mutual Aſpects, Sun and Moon's Riſing and Setting, Length of Days, Time of High Water, Fairs, Courts, and obſervable Days.

Fitted to the Latitude of Forty Degrees, and a Meridian of Five Hours Weſt from *London*, but may without ſenſible Error, ſerve all the adjacent Places, even from *Newfoundland* to *South-Carolina*.

By *RICHARD SAUNDERS*, Philom.

PHILADELPHIA:
Printed and ſold by *B. FRANKLIN*, at the New Printing-Office near the Market.

and the first library in the colonies. He designed the city's street lamps and founded a society to promote scientific research. He played an important role in creating Philadelphia's first hospital and the Academy for the Education of Youth, which became the University of Pennsylvania. During the Revolutionary War, Franklin traveled to France and won important military aid for America's cause. Franklin was 81 when the U.S. Constitution was being drawn up in 1787, and his good-humored patience helped cool heated arguments. When Franklin died in 1790, the United States lost one of its leading citizens.

Chapter FOUR

Revolution

IN APRIL 1775, TENSION BETWEEN THE COLON-
ists and the British army finally erupted into
war. Shots were fired at
Concord and Lexing-
ton in Massachusetts.

In Philadelphia,
this news inspired ordi-
nary citizens to be-
come soldiers. Some
were ready to fight
against the British,
some with the British,
and some weren't sure.
Some of Philadelphia's
leaders believed the
British government
needed to treat the

*Most soldiers in the
Continental army
were average citizens
willing to fight for the
freedom to determine
their own laws.*

colonists better. But they didn't want to fight the British. They were wealthy and had much to lose if a revolution failed and Britain punished the rebels. Couldn't they discuss this without fighting?

No! said the Patriots. They were ready for war. It was time to choose sides.

One year earlier, representatives from the colonies had formed the Continental Congress in Philadelphia. The representatives met to talk about problems with the British. In June 1775, the Continental Congress met again in Philadelphia. They asked George Washington to lead an American army against the British. In 1776, a newcomer to Philadelphia, Thomas Paine, wrote a pamphlet called *Common Sense.* It inspired people all over the colonies to support a revolution. In July, the Continental Congress approved the Declaration of Independence.

Pennsylvania's Patriots declared their independence, too. They ignored the proprietor's

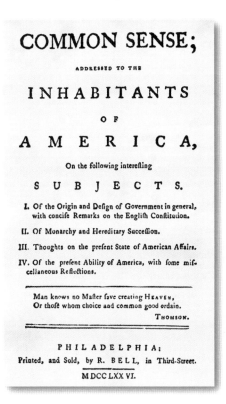

Thomas Paine's pamphlet Common Sense *inspired many colonists to fight for independence from Great Britain.*

25

George Washington led his troops across the Delaware River to New Jersey, where they won an important battle against the British.

government and formed a new one. They wrote a new state constitution.

Everyone in America waited to see what Britain would do next. King George III wasn't going to let the colonies go without a fight. Philadelphia was one of the British army's first targets. Washington marched his troops there to protect the city.

On the cold, snowy night of December 25, 1776, Washington and his troops snuck across the Delaware River from Pennsylvania into New Jersey. In the morning, they surprised a sleepy camp full of German soldiers, who were helping the British. Washington won an important victory there.

In late summer of 1777, the British landed in Maryland and marched north toward Philadelphia. Washington's army barely escaped to Chester, just outside Philadelphia. Britain's general, William Howe, entered the city in September. He was greeted by cheers from thousands of Tories. Tories were Americans who supported the British. Howe's officers spent a comfortable winter in Philadelphia.

Washington took his ragged, hungry troops to Valley Forge, northwest of Philadelphia. Farther west, dozens of American troops were injured or killed in a battle near the town of Paoli. It was a rough winter for the American army.

But in 1778 came some good news. Thanks to Benjamin Franklin's visit to France, the French would help the American army. The British left Philadelphia, fearing the French would come up the Delaware River and attack. That summer, American soldiers suffered another defeat in western Pennsylvania, this time at the hands of the Iroquois and the British. Soon after, American general John Sullivan took 5,000 men north from Easton, Pennsylvania, into New York. They destroyed 40 Iroquois villages and their crops. After

As this cartoon shows, colonial Patriots both young and old had little respect for "Tories," those Americans loyal to the king of England.

this, many Iroquois were forced into Canada.

The Revolutionary War soon moved away from Pennsylvania. But the state still made important contributions to the struggle. Thousands of Pennsylvania soldiers fought in battles around the colonies. Philadelphia businessmen such as Robert Morris helped pay for the army's supplies. Pennsylvania craftspeople made rifles. Ironworkers made cannons and cannonballs. Farmers grew crops to feed the huge army. Hospitals were set up for wounded soldiers in towns settled by a German religious group called the Moravians.

Robert Morris was a Philadelphia businessman who helped the American army purchase supplies during the Revolutionary War. After the war he served as the U.S. Superintendent of Finance and later became a U.S. senator from Pennsylvania.

In 1783, the war officially ended. The colonies were now independent. For a few years, the Continental Congress tried to run the country with laws it wrote called the **Articles of Confederation.** But it wasn't working. Many believed the new **federal** government was too weak. Once again, Americans would gather in Philadelphia to try to build a stronger nation.

THE WINTER GEORGE WASHINGTON AND HIS MEN SPENT AT VALLEY FORGE IN Pennsylvania was a turning point in the Revolution. At first, it looked bleak. December 1777 was an unusually cold month. Food and warm clothing were in short supply. Many Pennsylvania merchants and farmers preferred selling food and supplies to the British, who could pay in gold. The Americans' paper money was almost worthless.

Men began giving up and leaving the army. But in January, the weather became milder. A German army officer, Baron Friedrich Wilhelm von Steuben, arrived and trained the Americans to be better soldiers. Patriots also began giving the men at Valley Forge food and clothing. Then, in February, came the news that France would be providing soldiers and supplies.

Things hadn't looked good when Washington's army set up camp at Valley Forge. But when the winter ended, they were ready to keep fighting—and win—the war.

Chapter FIVE

A New Nation

In 1787, delegates from each state met at Independence Hall in Philadelphia in order to discuss revising the Articles of Confederation.

THE NEW UNITED STATES OF AMERICA WAS struggling. Its economy was weak, and states were arguing over boundaries. The federal government had no power to tax. Each state was supposed to send money to Congress to help run the government, but few did. States made their own agreements with foreign countries, causing more problems. There were no laws to govern what the states did.

In 1787, **delegates** from the states met in Philadelphia to discuss these problems. The goal was to make the

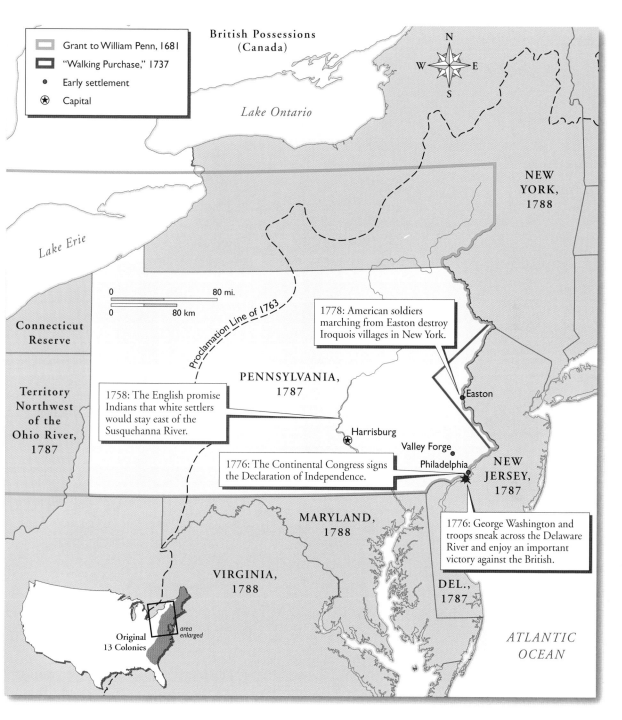

Grant to William Penn, 1681

"Walking Purchase," 1737

Early settlement

Capital

Lake Ontario

NEW
YORK,
1788

Lake Erie

0   80 mi.

0   80 km

1778: American soldiers
marching from Easton destroy
Iroquois villages in New York.

Connecticut
Reserve

Territory
Northwest
of the
Ohio River,
1787

1758: The English promise
Indians that white settlers
would stay east of the
Susquehanna River.

Proclamation Line of 1763

PENNSYLVANIA,
1787

Easton

Harrisburg

Valley Forge

1776: The Continental Congress signs
the Declaration of Independence.

Philadelphia

NEW
JERSEY,
1787

1776: George Washington and
troops sneak across the Delaware
River and enjoy an important
victory against the British.

MARYLAND,
1788

VIRGINIA,
1788

Original
13 Colonies

area
enlarged

DEL.,
1787

ATLANTIC
OCEAN

Articles of Confederation stronger. Instead,
the delegates decided to write a whole new
set of laws—a new federal constitution.

*Pennsylvania Colony
before statehood*

THE

FEDERALIST:

ADDRESSED TO THE

PEOPLE OF THE STATE OF NEW-YORK.

NUMBER I.

Introduction.

AFTER an unequivocal experience of the ineffi- cacy of the subsisting federal government, you are called upon to deliberate on a new constitution for the United States of America. The subject speaks its own importance; comprehending in its consequences, nothing less than the existence of the UNION, the safety and welfare of the parts of which it is com- posed, the fate of an empire, in many respects, the most interesting in the world. It has been frequently remarked, that it seems to have been reserved to the people of this country, by their conduct and example, to decide the important question, whether societies of men are really capable or not, of establishing good government from reflection and choice, or whether they are forever destined to depend, for their political constitutions, on accident and force. If there be any truth in the remark, the crisis, at which we are arrived, may with propriety be regarded as the æra in which

A   that

Those who wanted a constitu- tion that would create a strong national govern- ment were called Federalists. Those who wanted each state to have the freedom to do what it wanted were known as Anti-Federalists.

Pennsylvania's eight delegates were led by Benjamin Franklin, now 81 years old. Pennsylvania's Federalists—includ- ing James Wilson, Robert Morris, and Gouverneur Morris—were from Philadel- phia. Pennsylvania's Anti-Federalists tended to be from the western part of the state. They had never liked being told what to do by any government.

Pennsylvanians contributed much to the discussion about a new federal government. Though Franklin didn't vote, he helped settle arguments and urged all the delegates to keep working when they disagreed. James Wilson helped Virginia's James Madison write most of the Constitution's laws. Gouverneur Morris wrote the final draft of the Constitution. He changed the beginning to read "We, the people." He thought it was important for everyone in the United States to realize that the Constitution was for them.

Nine states had to approve the Constitution to make it the law of the land. All

Gouverneur Morris wrote the final draft of the Constitution.

33

across the country, people argued for or against the Constitution. The debate centered on whether or not a strong national government was good for Americans. Yes! argued the Federalists, because it would state what people's rights were and would protect them. No! said the Anti-Federalists, because the country would be run by a few people who wouldn't care what the different states need.

In the end, the Federalists won the argument. In December 1787, Pennsylvania became the second state to approve the Constitution. In time, all 13 states approved the Constitution. Many states were

A parade celebrating the 200th anniversary of the U.S. Constitution passes in front of Independence Hall in Philadelphia, Pennsylvania.

persuaded to approve when they were promised that the **Bill of Rights** would be added. This guaranteed the rights of individuals such as freedom of speech.

A statue of William Penn sits atop Philadelphia's City Hall as a lasting tribute to Penn and his belief in equality for all people.

Some historians have said that William Penn and the Quakers, with their strong belief in equal rights for all people, built the foundation for the country. Today, the U.S. Constitution, which promises those equal rights, has lasted longer than any other among major world nations. Pennsylvanians can be proud of their state's contribution to the United States of America.

Interesting Fact

▶ The Liberty Bell was taken out of Philadelphia in 1777 to keep it from harm by the British. When it was returned to the city in June 1778, a train of 700 wagons escorted it.

1500s   Many Native American groups, including the Lenni-Lenape, Nanticoke, Shawnee, Susquehanna, and Erie, live in what is now Pennsylvania.

1638   Sweden starts Pennsylvania's first European settlement.

1655   The Dutch gain control of the Delaware Bay region.

1681   William Penn receives a charter for Pennsylvania.

1701   William Penn writes Pennsylvania's constitution.

1737   In the "walking purchase," Thomas Penn cheats the Lenni-Lenape out of much of their land.

1758   The British promise Native Americans that white settlers would stay east of the Susquehanna River.

1763   The British defeat the French in the French and Indian War. The British tell Pennsylvania settlers they must obey the 1758 agreement with the Native Americans.

1765   Parliament passes the Stamp Act, a new tax on printed goods; colonists protest, and the tax is ended.

1775   The American Revolution begins.

1776   While meeting in Philadelphia, the Continental Congress adopts the Declaration of Independence; soon after, Pennsylvania forms a new state government and rewrites its constitution. In December, George Washington leads his troops from Pennsylvania to a victory in New Jersey.

1777   The British take over Philadelphia; Washington's troops spend a cold, hard winter at Valley Forge.

1783   The Revolutionary War ends, and the United States becomes an independent country.

1787   The U.S. Constitution is created in Philadelphia.

Glossary Terms

Articles of Confederation
(AR-tik-uhls uv kon-fed-uh-RAY-shun)
The Articles of Confederation was the first constitution of the United States. It was replaced by the U.S. Constitution in 1788.

assembly (uh-SEM-blee)
An assembly is a lawmaking part of government. William Penn set up a general assembly for Pennsylvania made up of representatives from around the colony.

Bill of Rights (BILL uv RITES)
The Bill of Rights is a list of individual rights that are protected, such as freedom of speech and freedom of religion. The Bill of Rights is the first 10 amendments, or changes, to the U.S. Constitution.

boycotting (BOY-kot-ing)
When people are boycotting something, they are refusing to buy a certain product. The colonists boycotted English products to protest taxes.

charter (CHAR-tuhr)
A charter is a document giving someone permission to set up a colony. King Charles II gave William Penn a charter for Pennsylvania in 1681.

constitution (kon-stuh-TOO-shun)
A constitution is a document setting up a govern-ment. The U.S. Constitution was written in Philadelphia in 1787.

Continental Congress
(kon-tuh-NENT-uhl KON-griss)
The Continental Congress was a meeting of colonists that served as the American government during Revolutionary times. The Continental Congress adopted the Declaration of Independence in Philadelphia in 1776.

delegates (DEL-uh-guhts)
Delegates are people who represent other people at a meeting. At the meeting to write the U.S. Constitution, Pennsylvania delegate Gouverneur Morris changed the beginning to read, "We, the people."

federal (FED-uh-ruhl)
Something is federal if it has to do with the national government. Under the Articles of Confederation, the federal government was very weak.

longhouse (LONG-hows)
A longhouse a large Native American building made of a wooden frame covered by bark. Many Lenni-Lenape lived together in one longhouse.

pamphlets (PAM-flets)
Pamphlets are printed booklets with no cover. William Penn sent pamphlets around Europe encouraging people to move to Pennsylvania.

Parliament (PAR-luh-muhnt)
Parliament is the lawmaking part of the British government. In 1765, Parliament began passing taxes on the colonies, angering colonists.

George Clymer (1739–1813)

Continental Congress delegate, 1776–77, 1780–82; Declaration of Independence signer; Constitutional Convention delegate, 1787; U.S. Constitution signer; Pennsylvania legislature member, 1781–96

Thomas FitzSimons (1739–1811)

Constitutional Convention delegate, 1787; U.S. Constitution signer; U.S. House of Representatives member, 1789–95

Benjamin Franklin (1706–1790)

Agent in Europe for Pennsylvania, 1764–75, and later for Pennsylvania, Georgia, New Jersey, Massachusetts; Continental Congress delegate, 1775; Declaration of Independence; Pennsylvania supreme executive council president, 1785–87; Constitutional Convention senior member, 1787; U.S. Constitution signer

Jared Ingersoll (1749–1822)

Continental Congress delegate, 1780–81; Constitutional Convention delegate, 1787; U.S. Constitution signer

Thomas Mifflin (1744–1800)

Continental Congress delegate, 1774–76, 1782–84; Continental Congress president, 1783; Constitutional Convention delegate, 1787; U.S. Constitution signer; Pennsylvania governor, 1790–99

Robert Morris (1734–1806)

Continental Congress delegate, 1775–78; Declaration of Independence signer; Articles of Confederation signer; author of the plan for a National Bank, 1781; Constitutional Convention delegate, 1787; U.S. Constitution signer; U.S. senator, 1789–95

Joseph Reed (1741–1785)

Pennsylvania supreme executive council president, 1778–81; Articles of Confederation signer

George Ross (1730–1779)

Continental Congress delegate, 1774–77; Declaration of Independence signer

Benjamin Rush (1745–1813)

Continental Congress delegate, 1776–77; Declaration of Independence signer

Jonathan Bayard Smith (1742–1812)

Congress delegate, 1777; Articles of Confederation signer

James Wilson (1742–1798)

Continental Congress, 1775–77, 1782, 1785–87; Declaration of Independence signer; Constitutional Convention signer, 1787; U.S. Constitution signer

Web Sites

Visit our homepage for lots of links about the Pennsylvania colony:
http://www.childsworld.com/links.html

Note to Parents, Teachers, and Librarians:
We routinely verify our Web links to make sure they're safe,
active sites—so encourage your readers to check them out!

Books

Furgang, Kathy. *The Declaration of Independence and Benjamin Franklin of Pennsylvania.* New York: PowerKids Press, 2002.

Heinrichs, Ann. *Pennsylvania.* Danbury, Conn.: Children's Press, 2000.

Knight, James. *Seventh and Walnut: Life in Colonial Philadelphia.* Mahwah, N.J.: Troll Communications, 1999.

Lutz, Norma Jean. *William Penn: Founder of Democracy.* Broomall, Pa.: Chelsea House, 2000.

Places to Visit or Contact

Historical Society of Pennsylvania
To find out more about Pennsylvania history
1300 Locust Street
Philadelphia, PA 19107
215/732-6200

Independence Hall
To see where the Continental Congress declared independence from Great Britain and where the U.S. Constitution was written
Chestnut Street
Philadelphia, PA 19103
215/597-8974

Index

About the Author

JEAN KINNEY WILLIAMS LIVES AND WRITES IN CINCINNATI, OHIO. Her nonfiction books for children include *Matthew Henson: Polar Adventurer* and a series of books about American religions, which include *The Amish, The Shakers, The Mormons, The Quakers,* and *The Christian Scientists.* She is also the author of *The Pony Express* and *African-Americans in the Colonies.*